INSTANT NUMEROLOGY

SANDRA KOVACS STEIN

Foreword by Kevin Quinn Avery, D.Ms.

Introduction by Matthew Oliver Goodwin

NEWCASTLE PUBLISHING CO., INC.

NORTH HOLLYWOOD, CALIFORNIA

1986

To my children—Joanne and Howard

LIBRARY OF CONGRESS CATALOG CARD NUMBER: 78-24697
ISBN: 0-87877-089-5

Designed by C. Linda Dingler
Cover Design: Riley K. Smith

A NEWCASTLE BOOK
10 9 8 7 6 5 4 3

Printed in the United States of America

CONTENTS

ACKNOWLEDGMENTS

My sincere thanks to Kevin Quinn Avery for giving me the incentive to write this book, and to Frank William Vilen for his suggestions concerning the work sheet and for the use of his name and birth date in setting up the charts.

FOREWORD

by Kevin Quinn Avery, D.Ms.

It is my great pleasure to write this introduction for Sandra Stein, who has presented in this text a valid basic introduction into the sacred science of numbers.

The history of numbers is as old as the recorded history of man. Numerology was in use in ancient Greece, Rome, Egypt, and China and is to be found in the ancient books of wisdom, such as the Hebrew Kabala. Its origins go even further beyond into the temples of Isis, Atlantis, and Lemuria.

Numerology is interlocked with the other so-called occult sciences—astrology, the tarot, the *I Ching,* and so on. From each is learned a little that represents the whole. All are interrelated. Each complements the others, with all being equally true. There is really no necessity for entering on a long discourse on the antiquity of astrology and/or numerology. Both commenced when man first gazed upon the heavens, noting the

---

Kevin Quinn Avery, D.Ms., a professional numerologist, is author of *The Numbers of Life, The Cycle of Man, The Age of Aetherius,* and *The Magic Light.*

movements of the celestial bodies. The planets move to the melodious rhythm of mathematical precision, and numerology itself is an offshoot of the planetary movements. One could not exist without the other.

Of all the occult sciences, numerology is the most spiritual. The word *spiritual* is employed here as it relates to inner growth. The forecasting part is easy. It is not difficult for an advanced astrologer/numerologist to tell how, when, or where. It is the *why* that is important. It is this *why* in which numerology excels.

All the occult sciences are tied into reincarnation and karma. It is not necessary for the reader to believe in either one for the science to work for him, but those who do adhere to these cosmic laws will achieve a better understanding.

All of us follow a life path that is predestined. We cannot bring anything into life that is not predestined, nor can we reject anything that is. Where our free will comes into play is in how we handle what we are presented with. We have the free will to choose to handle situations positively or negatively. Someday man will learn that the total freedom of the stars comes when he elects to surrender his petty freedom to act negatively in order to gain total freedom.

Both the undertones and overtones of numerology and any of the other metaphysical sciences are extremely spiritual. They answer the question of where we come from, where we are going, and, more important, what we are doing here and what is expected of us. The beauty of knowing these aspects is to push the positive and pull away from the negative, thus creating a much smoother and more successful life.

There exists a law that governs the universe. Order and direction are maintained upon this earth. Very little is left to chance, and control is maintained by the firmly established, unalterable influences of the law of karma, which in turn is tied into the cycle of rebirth, or incarnations. This is the cosmic law, which does not bend to accommodate man's whims. This earth is nothing but a classroom, and what I refer to as the God-Force has all eternity to play the game, and in the end will be the winner.

There are two things never promised anyone in life. The first is happiness, the second is unhappiness. However, to a large extent, whether one is happy or unhappy depends on how we relate to the lessons we are on this earth to learn.

Life, in essence, is very simple. We live this life to grow, to manifest, and to achieve spiritual knowledge and universal love. Each individual is dealing with a different type of lesson. What is easy for one is difficult for another. The overall destiny or life path will lead the individual into the aspects of these lessons. Those who follow the easy path and pull away will bring upon themselves their own unhappiness. Those who embrace the lessons will find the opposite. Perhaps it can be put a much simpler way: whatever the big personality defect of any individual at birth may be, this is the very thing that will be the overall destiny. For example, those who might have a lesson in overcoming the fear of poverty will, almost categorically, be born into destitution. Only by living with this destitution will they be able to overcome the fear of it. Those who do overcome this fear will shortly leave the poverty for abundance. Those who do not will spend their entire lives and many other countless lives laboring with this destitution until the fear is lost. Perhaps an oversimplification, but nonetheless an example of the basic purpose of karma and reincarnation.

The study of numerology as it advances into a study of numbers and kabalistic interpretations provides the insight into why any individual is living this particular life—what lessons he is dealing with. This knowledge enables one to overcome the negative and exchange it for the positive.

There is *no* set meaning to any single number. They all have positive and/or negative aspects. The same number can mean peace or war. It depends upon what is operating with it, and whether the individual himself is either positive or negative.

There is no need to pursue this direction in this text. What Sandra Stein is presenting is a basic introduction into numerology to enable the reader to begin to assess his own life and to begin to get an understanding of his or her destiny. This is a good foundational text, a concrete base for those who choose to continue the study.

It was my intent via this introduction to present some of the deeper meanings of the science. Sandra Stein has divorced the spiritual undercurrents from her presentation of the science so as to enable the reader to gain an occult-free introduction.

May the blessings of the eternal God-Force be with you.

Kevin Quinn Avery
New York City
June 1978

INTRODUCTION

Numerology is, without question, the easiest of the occult fields to learn. The calculations require only the simplest arithmetic and the interpretations derive from the symbolic meaning of only eleven different quantities—the numbers 1, 2, 3, 4, 5, 6, 7, 8, 9, 11 and 22. If you can add and if you can work with eleven simple definitions, you have the complete basis for this exciting field.

What can you do with numerology? On one level, numerology can be used to read people's characters and to understand the opportunities and influences present in people's lives at any given time. On a broader level, numerology defines the deeper lessons which a person is learning. It can relate the growth of the soul in this lifetime to past growth and future potential in a meaningful demonstration of the laws of reincarnation. On a higher level still, numerology illuminates religious and metaphysical studies and contributes to an understanding of the universe and its complexities.

The origins of numerology go back many centuries, at least to Pythagoras in the sixth century B.C., probably even farther back to the peoples of ancient Egypt, China or India. At some time in pre-history, man first derived the fundamentals of numerology, either by observation, meditation, divine inspiration, or most likely, a combination of all three. Over the intervening centuries, numerologists have continued to observe people, along with their characteristics and motivations. The findings of the original numerologists have been checked and refined in the field countless times, confirming over a period of thousands of years the vital correlations between people's traits and the numbers which numerologists assign to these traits.

Most numerologists relate to the divine, mystically inspired origin and nature of their special field. I accept that understanding, but I also appreciate the part that observation and analysis have played in numerology's development. It's true that numerology loses some of the mystery surrounding it if we accept experiential observation and deduction as part of its basis. By virtue of this observation and deduction, however, the field of numerology gains the solidity usually associated with other disciplines based on careful analytical study.

In ancient times, numerology and its sister arts were the province of priests or wise men who emphasized the mystical nature of their work and carefully withheld most of their information from the general public. Today, numerology and the other occult fields are completely accessible to those who are interested. There are many fine books available for study, including the one you're holding in your hand right now.

Beginning books in the occult fields have often been a source of annoyance to me. Some of them are so simplified as to distort the subject matter. Some, on the other hand, attempt to be so all-inclusive as to frighten off the potential reader. I'm delighted to be introducing Sandra Kovacs Stein's book which provides a happy balance I appreciate. There's a lot of information here—and it's the real stuff. It's presented and explained clearly and concisely so that you can make use of it immediately. When you read this book, you'll probably understand yourself better and you'll find a new understanding of others in your life as well. You'll develop a good foundation for character reading and an understanding of the present forces in your life and others' lives. If you don't read any other numerology books after you complete this book, you'll still find that you have a useful new tool at your disposal. If you choose to move forward with advanced studies, you'll find that *Instant Numerology* has given you a firm and accurate foundation on which to build.

Matthew Oliver Goodwin
Los Angeles, 1985

PREFACE

Life is a manifestation of energy. Everything in our universe has its own vibration—moving in a certain way, moving at a certain speed. We are all affected by these vibrations and must learn to work with them rather than against them. How we can best do this, however, is different for each one of us. We must harmonize our personal vibrations to those of the universe, and although we are all made up of the same elements, they are present in different and unique combinations. No two people are ever exactly alike.

Numerology is a charting device that describes your own personal vibrations as determined by your birth date and the name you were given at birth. It is a way of describing how your energies have operated in the past, how they are operating now, and how they are most likely to operate in the future—unless you decide to handle them in a different way. Forewarned is forearmed. When you are unaware of the forces in your life, you are at their mercy. Once you recognize them for what they are, you can direct them and take full responsibility for your life. To give you an exaggerated example, it is like knowing that you don't have to freeze to death just because the weather is turning cold, or that you don't have to drown just because you happen to be standing on the beach when the tide starts to come in.

Numerology can best be used as a road map to help you plan your life. In addition to showing you what influences, opportunities, and obstacles are operating at any given time, it shows you which roads are open to you and where each one is likely to lead. Use it to find the best route to take you where you want to go!

To study and understand numerology completely can be a long and complicated business. However, the purpose of this book is to simplify things for the reader who hasn't the time or the inclination to master the science himself. This is a very basic step-by-step instruction book for those who want instant results—those who would like to set up and interpret a chart "immediately" without having to attend a class or do any amount of reading first. By no means does it cover the entire topic of numerology. It is only a taste.

For those of you who having tasted would like to delve further into the subject, I highly recommend the following two books:

The Numbers of Life, by Kevin Quinn Avery, published by Doubleday & Co. (Dolphin Books), Garden City, New York, 1977.

Numerology, The Complete Guide, Vols. I and II, by Matthew Oliver Goodwin, published by Newcastle Publishing Co., North Hollywood, CA, 1981.

Symbols of Numerology, by Julia Seton, M.D., published by Newcastle Publishing Co., North Hollywood, CA, 1984.

Your Days Are Numbered, by Florence Campbell, published by The Gateway, Ferndale, PA, 1976.

PART I

SETTING UP YOUR CHART

A numerology chart is a personalized aid to help you plan your life more intelligently by telling you facts about yourself and your destiny that can help you live up to your full potential and get the most out of life. It uses two sets of numbers—one set derived from your name, and the other from your birth date.

The numbers in your name describe your personality, your inner self, what makes you tick, how others see you, and where your hidden talents lie.

The numbers in your birth date describe the environment you will be exposed to at different times in your life, the opportunities you will have, and the obstacles you are likely to face.

It is the combination of the two together—name and birth date—that is unique. Many people can share your birth date, and some people may even have the same name. But *you* are the only person in the whole world who has that particular combination, which is why no two lives are ever exactly the same.

To do a numerology chart you need two pieces of information:

1. Your full name *exactly* as it appears on your birth certificate. (If you have no birth certificate, you should use the name you have always been known by.)
2. Your date of birth.

Turn the page to see what a numerology chart looks like.

1	A	J	S
2	B	K	T
3	C	L	U
4	D	M	V
5	E	N	W
6	F	O	X
7	G	P	Y
8	H	Q	Z
9	I	R	

Letter values

line 1
Vowels

line 2
Name

line 3
Consonants

line 4
Total

box A

1	
2	
3	
4	
5	
6	
7	
8	
9	

Total letters in
each number

box B

Karmic lessons

line 5

Month

Day

Year of Birth

box E

Destiny
number

box F

Life cycles   Years

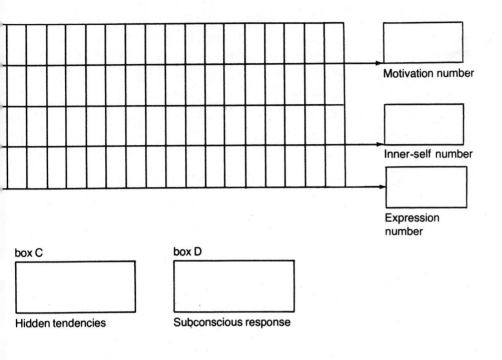

Motivation number

Inner-self number

Expression number

box C

Hidden tendencies

box D

Subconscious response

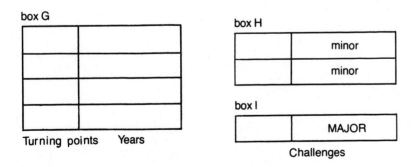

box G

Turning points   Years

box H

	minor
	minor

box I

	MAJOR

Challenges

1

YOUR NAME

Start by entering your full name on line 2 of the work sheet. It must be entered *exactly* as it appears on the birth certificate, even if it is misspelled, incomplete, wrong, or recorded merely as *Baby Smith* or *Girl Jones*. The only thing you do *not* use is the word *Jr.* or *II* or *III* if it follows the name.

As mentioned at the beginning of this chapter, the name at your birth describes your personality—what you came into this world with, who you are, what you really want and need, how you react, where your strengths and weaknesses lie. These things can *not* be altered by a new name. You never lose what you were born with. When you change your name you attract new vibrations to yourself, which usually show where you are placing the emphasis at this time of your life. When a name change has been properly planned, it can act as an external aid to help promote the success and speed up the opportunities that have been promised at birth. For example, if you take on a name with strong artistic vibrations, it will not make you an artist unless there are artistic talents evident in your own originally recorded name. What the new name can do is lead you into artistic associations and create a market for your wares, which would be of great benefit if you happen to be an artist but of little value to you otherwise.

Since you are going to be working with numbers, the letters of the name must be converted into numerical values using the following code:

1	2	3	4	5	6	7	8	9
A	B	C	D	E	F	G	H	I
J	K	L	M	N	O	P	Q	R
S	T	U	V	W	X	Y	Z	

To start, we will figure out your motivation, inner-self, and expression numbers. To do this, first write the numerical value for each vowel in the name on line 1 (above the name). Write the numerical value for each consonant in the name on line 3 (below the name). Write the numerical value for each letter in the name (both consonants and vowels) on line 4.

As an example, I will use the name FRANK WILLIAM VILEN.

line 1 Vowels		1				9		9	1			9		5					
line 2 Name	F	R	A	N	K	W	I	L	L	I	A	M	V	I	L	E	N		
line 3 Consonants	6	9		5	2	5		3	3			4	4		3		5		
line 4 Total	6	9	1	5	2	5	9	3	3	9	1	4	4	9	3	5	5		

MOTIVATION NUMBER

The motivation number describes the motive behind the decisions you make and the way you act. It is what makes you tick.

To get the motivation number, add up all the numbers on line 1 (vowels) and write the total in the box labeled "Motivation number" at the end of line 1. If the sum is larger than 9, it must be reduced. This is because in numerology we work with the numbers 1 through 9, 11, and 22. Any number larger than 9 (except 11 and 22) must be reduced by adding the digits together. If the sum of the digits is larger than 9, it must be reduced again. For example,

$$1978 \ (1 + 9 + 7 + 8) = 25 \ (2 + 5) = 7.$$
$$92 \ (9 + 2) = 11. \ (\text{Remember, 11 and 22 do not get reduced further.})$$

Frank William Vilen's motivation number is 7:

line 1 Vowels		1				9		9 1			9	5		→	7

Motivation number

$$1 + 9 + 9 + 1 + 9 + 5 = 34 \ (3 + 4) = 7.$$

INNER-SELF NUMBER

The inner-self number reveals what your secret dreams are made of, how the inner person within you pictures yourself (sometimes without even realizing it). It is also quite often the first impression other people obtain of you before they actually get to know you.

To get the inner-self number, add up all the numbers on line 3 (consonants). Write the reduced total in the box labeled "Inner-self number" at the end of line 3.

Frank William Vilen's inner-self number is 4.

line 3 Consonants	6	9	5	2	5	3	3		4	4	3	5	→	4

Inner-self number

$$6 + 9 + 5 + 2 + 5 + 3 + 3 + 4 + 4 + 3 + 5 = 49 \ (4 + 9) = 13 \ (3 + 1) = 4.$$

EXPRESSION NUMBER

The expression number describes how you interact with other people. It tells how you best express yourself in life and where your talents lie.

To get the expression number, add up all the numbers on line 4 (the total of both the consonants and the vowels in the name). Write the reduced total in the box labeled "Expression number" at the end of line 4.

Frank William Vilen's expression number is 11. (Remember, 11 does not get reduced further.)

line 4 Total																	Expression number
6	9	1	5	2	5	9	3	3	9	1	4	4	9	3	5	5	11

$6 + 9 + 1 + 5 + 2 + 5 + 9 + 3 + 3 + 9 + 1 + 4 + 4 + 9 + 3 + 5 + 5 = 83$
$(8 + 3) = 11$.

Now look at line 4 (Total) again, and count how many letters fall into each numerical category. Write each total in the appropriate section of box A.

Frank William Vilen has seventeen letters in his name. Two of these letters have a numerical value of 1, one has a numerical value of 2, three have a numerical value of 3, two have a numerical value of 4, four have a numerical value of 5, one has a numerical value of 6, and four have a numerical value of 9.

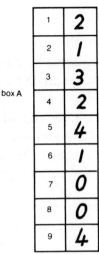

box A

1	2
2	1
3	3
4	2
5	4
6	1
7	0
8	0
9	4

Total letters in
each number

KARMIC LESSONS

The karmic lessons describe the things you are supposed to learn in this life.

Each numerical category that has no letters in it represents a karmic lesson that needs to be learned. Look at box A and see which numerical categories have a 0 next to them. Write these numbers in box B, labeled "Karmic lessons."

Frank William Vilen has no 7s or 8s in his name.

box B

7, 8

Karmic lessons

HIDDEN TENDENCIES

The hidden tendencies describe desires to which you have been exposed in the past. Because of their overemphasis in your chart, they must be watched so that you do not go overboard with them.

Again look at box A. Any numerical category that has 4 or more letters in it represents a hidden tendency to which you have already been exposed. Write these numbers in box C, labeled "Hidden tendencies."

Frank William Vilen has four letters in category 5, and four letters in category 9.

box C

Hidden tendencies

SUBCONSCIOUS RESPONSE

The subconscious-response number tells how you instinctively and automatically react when faced with an emergency situation.

To find the subconscious-response number, subtract the amount of karmic lessons to be learned from the number 9. Write the result in box D, labeled "Subconscious-response number."

Frank William Vilen has two karmic lessons to learn. $9 - 2 = 7$. His subconscious response number is 7.

box D

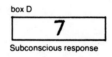

Subconscious response

2

YOUR BIRTH DATE

Your birth date describes the influences, opportunities, and obstacles that will be present during your life. It can show you what alternatives are available to you and what the probable outcome of each will be.

Enter the birth date on line 5.

Frank William Vilen was born on May 8, 1941.

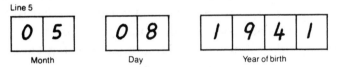

Line 5

| 0 | 5 | | 0 | 8 | | 1 | 9 | 4 | 1 |

Month   Day   Year of birth

DESTINY NUMBER

Your destiny number is one of the most important numbers in your chart—it is the ruling force that describes what you *must* do in order to operate harmoniously with your environment and get the most out of your life.

The destiny number is the reduced sum of the birth month, the birth day, and the birth year. Write this number in box E, labeled "Destiny number."

Frank William Vilen was born on May 8, 1941. He has a destiny number of 1. $5 + 8 + 1941 = 1954$ $(1 + 9 + 5 + 4) = 19$ $(1 + 9) = 10$ $(1 + 0) = 1$.

box E

Destiny
number

LIFE CYCLES

The life cycles represent the circumstances and conditions you will be exposed to at certain times during your life. Just as your birth date is divided into three numbers (month, day, year), so too is your life divided into three major cycles.

First Cycle. The number of the first cycle is the reduced number of the month of birth. This cycle lasts from your birth until you reach maturity. (A simplified way of finding out when you reach maturity and end the first cycle is to subtract your destiny number from the number 36 and then add a 1 to the result.) The calendar year of your maturity is your birth year plus your age of maturity.

On the top line of box F write the number of the first cycle, the year it started, and the year it ends.

Frank William Vilen was born in May. His first life-cycle number is a 5. Frank matured at age 36 ($36 - 1 = 35$. $35 + 1 = 36$). His first life cy-

box F

5	1941–1977

Life cycles   Years

cle lasted from 1941 until 1977 (1941 + 36 = 1977).

Second Cycle. The number of your second cycle is the reduced number of the day of birth. This cycle starts at the end of the first cycle and lasts approximately 27 years (add 27 to the year the first cycle ends). On the middle line of box F write the number of the second cycle, the year it starts, and the year it ends.

Frank William Vilen was born on the eighth day of the month. His second cycle is an 8. It will last from 1977 until 2004 (1977 + 27 = 2004).

box F

8	**1977-2004**

Life cycles   Years

Third Cycle. The number of your third cycle is the reduced number of your year of birth. It starts at the end of the second cycle and lasts for the rest of your life. Write the number of the third cycle and the year it starts on the bottom line of box F.

Frank William Vilen was born in 1941. 1941 (1 + 9 + 4 + 1) = 15 (1 + 5) = 6. His third cycle is a 6. It will start in 2004 and will last to the end of his life.

box F

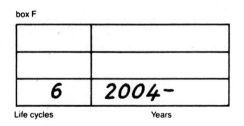

6	**2004-**

Life cycles   Years

TURNING POINTS

The turning points describe certain events that may occur during a given life cycle. There are four turning points.

First Turning Point. The first turning point is the reduced sum of the month and day of birth. It starts and ends at the same time that the first life cycle does.

Write the number of the first turning point, the year it started, and the year it ends on the first line of box G.

Frank William Vilen was born on May 8. $5 + 8 = 13 \ (1 + 3) = 4$. His first turning point is a 4. It will last from 1941 until 1977.

box G

4	*1941-1977*

Turning points   Years

Second Turning Point. The number of your second turning point is the reduced sum of the day and year of birth. This turning point starts at the end of the first turning point and lasts for nine years. Write the number of the second turning point, the year it starts, and the year it ends on the second line of box G.

Frank William Vilen was born on the eighth day of the month in 1941. $8 + 1941 = 1949 \ (1 + 9 + 4 + 9) = 23 \ (2 + 3) = 5$. His second turning point is a 5. It will last from 1977 to 1986 ($1977 + 9 = 1986$).

box G

5	*1977-1986*

Turning points   Years

Third Turning Point. **The number of your third turning point is the reduced sum of the first and second turning points. It starts at the end of the second turning point and lasts nine years.**

Write the number of the third turning point, the year it starts, and the year it ends on the third line of box G.

Frank William Vilen's third turning point is 9 (4 + 5 = 9). It will last from 1986 until 1995 (1986 + 9 = 1995).

box G

9	*1986-1995*

Turning points   Years

Fourth Turning Point. **The number of your fourth turning point is the reduced sum of the month and year of birth. It starts at the end of the third turning point and lasts for the rest of your life.**

Write the number of the fourth turning point and the year it starts on the bottom line of box G.

Frank William Vilen was born in May of 1941.   5 + 1941 = 1946

$(1 + 9 + 4 + 6) = 20 (2 + 0) = 2$. His fourth turning point is 2. It will last from 1995 to the end of his life.

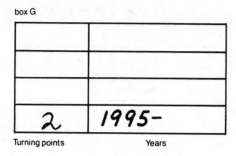

box G

2	1995–

Turning points   Years

CHALLENGES

The challenges are weaknesses to which you are prone. They are stumbling blocks that stand in your way. There are two minor challenges and one major one.

First Minor Challenge. To find the number of your first minor challenge, first reduce your day and month of birth and then subtract the smaller number from the larger one. Write this number on the top line of box H.

Frank William Vilen was born on May 8. $8 - 5 = 3$. His first minor challenge is 3.

box H

3	minor
	minor

Second Minor Challenge. To find the number of your second minor challenge, first reduce your day and year of birth and then subtract the smaller number from the larger one. Write this number on the bottom line of box H.

Frank William Vilen was born on the eighth day of the month in 1941. 8 − 6 = 2. His second minor challenge is 2.

box H

Major Challenge. To find the major challenge subtract the two minor challenges from each other. Write this number in box I.

Frank William Vilen's major challenge is 1 (3 − 2 = 1).

box I

| *1* | MAJOR |

Challenges

That is all there is to it! You have just set up a basic numerological chart. And now, if you turn to Part II—Interpreting the Chart—you will find out what all these numbers mean.

PART II

INTERPRETING
YOUR CHART

3

COMPATIBILITY OF NUMBERS

Throughout this section on interpretation, I shall be talking about certain numbers being in harmony or at odds with certain other numbers. This will hold true whether you are comparing two numbers in the same chart or two numbers belonging to two different people. Certain numbers get along well together, while certain other numbers create a conflict when combined. The importance of knowing this is that it can be used as a guide—your motivation number can be compared with your expression number to see if what you really want to do in life fits what you are actually doing; a life cycle can be compared with a turning point to see if there will be any conflict during that period; your destiny number can be compared to that of another person to see whether you are both following a compatible or conflicting path in life.

The simplest way of deciding whether two numbers are compatible or not is the system of "odds and evens." All the odd numbers (1, 3, 5, 7, 9, 11) get along harmoniously. All the even numbers (2, 4, 6, 8, 22) get along harmoniously. Combine an odd number with an even number, however, and there is bound to be some conflict.

4

MOTIVATION NUMBER

(line 1—total of vowels in name)

Note: If your motivation number and expression number are at odds, what you want to do may not fit what you are actually doing, or there may be constant interference in your life so that you feel frustrated at not being able to express what you really would like to.

If your motivation number is the same as your destiny number you will find it easy to get what you want. If, however, they are at odds, you will probably have trouble finding opportunities to express your real ideals.

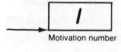

"1" is ambitious, dislikes detail, wants to lead, direct, dominate, be praised. "1" is concerned with his outer image. "1" prefers to be a loner.

"2" craves love and understanding. "2" would rather follow than lead. "2" wants partnerships, marriage, companionship, peace, harmony, and comfort.

24

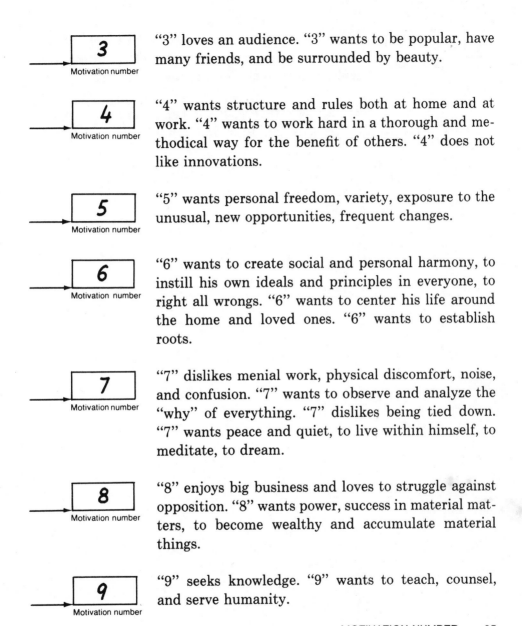

3 — Motivation number

"3" loves an audience. "3" wants to be popular, have many friends, and be surrounded by beauty.

4 — Motivation number

"4" wants structure and rules both at home and at work. "4" wants to work hard in a thorough and methodical way for the benefit of others. "4" does not like innovations.

5 — Motivation number

"5" wants personal freedom, variety, exposure to the unusual, new opportunities, frequent changes.

6 — Motivation number

"6" wants to create social and personal harmony, to instill his own ideals and principles in everyone, to right all wrongs. "6" wants to center his life around the home and loved ones. "6" wants to establish roots.

7 — Motivation number

"7" dislikes menial work, physical discomfort, noise, and confusion. "7" wants to observe and analyze the "why" of everything. "7" dislikes being tied down. "7" wants peace and quiet, to live within himself, to meditate, to dream.

8 — Motivation number

"8" enjoys big business and loves to struggle against opposition. "8" wants power, success in material matters, to become wealthy and accumulate material things.

9 — Motivation number

"9" seeks knowledge. "9" wants to teach, counsel, and serve humanity.

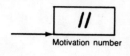

Motivation number

"11" is a visionary who wants to be surrounded by like people, who wants others to act according to his ideals, who prefers ideals to his fellow men.

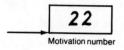

Motivation number

"22" is interested in the good and security of all mankind. "22" wants to build for humanity.

5

INNER-SELF NUMBER

(line 3—total of consonants in name)

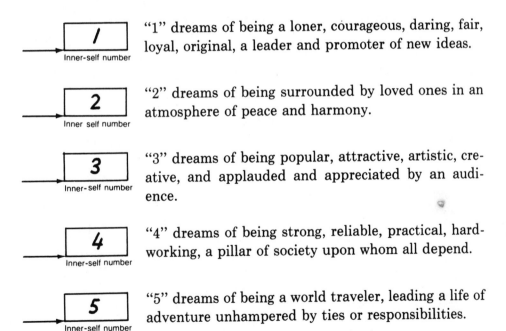

1 Inner-self number	"1" dreams of being a loner, courageous, daring, fair, loyal, original, a leader and promoter of new ideas.
2 Inner self number	"2" dreams of being surrounded by loved ones in an atmosphere of peace and harmony.
3 Inner-self number	"3" dreams of being popular, attractive, artistic, creative, and applauded and appreciated by an audience.
4 Inner-self number	"4" dreams of being strong, reliable, practical, hardworking, a pillar of society upon whom all depend.
5 Inner-self number	"5" dreams of being a world traveler, leading a life of adventure unhampered by ties or responsibilities.

27

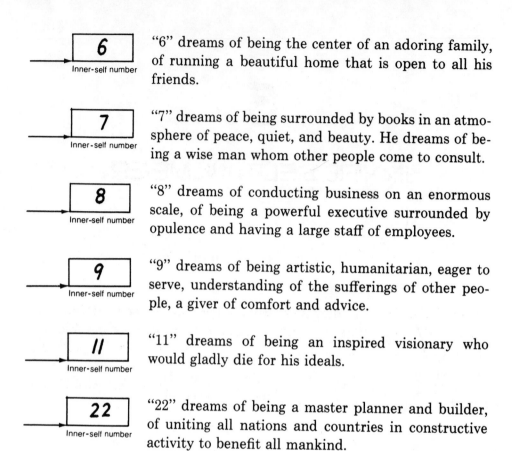

6 — Inner-self number

"6" dreams of being the center of an adoring family, of running a beautiful home that is open to all his friends.

7 — Inner-self number

"7" dreams of being surrounded by books in an atmosphere of peace, quiet, and beauty. He dreams of being a wise man whom other people come to consult.

8 — Inner-self number

"8" dreams of conducting business on an enormous scale, of being a powerful executive surrounded by opulence and having a large staff of employees.

9 — Inner-self number

"9" dreams of being artistic, humanitarian, eager to serve, understanding of the sufferings of other people, a giver of comfort and advice.

11 — Inner-self number

"11" dreams of being an inspired visionary who would gladly die for his ideals.

22 — Inner-self number

"22" dreams of being a master planner and builder, of uniting all nations and countries in constructive activity to benefit all mankind.

6

EXPRESSION NUMBER

(line 4—total of all letters in name)

Note: If your expression number and destiny number are harmonious, you will always find work you can do. If, however, they are at odds, you will have to make many adjustments and struggle to find a place for yourself.

If your expression number is the same as one of your karmic lessons, you will have some difficulty in your dealings with the world until that karmic lesson has been mastered.

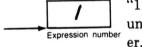

"1" is a nonconformist, daring, forceful, aggressive, unconventional, ambitious, creative, original, a leader. "1" is happiest being the boss, or doing work that leaves him unhampered to carry out his own ideas.

"2" brings harmony and love to family and group, often works behind the scenes, is cooperative, passive, shy, vulnerable, a sensitive sponge soaking in every detail of his environment. "2" is most at home in occupations in which he can work in association with other people, in which detail and minuteness are important, or in which he can put his innate tact and desire for harmony to use.

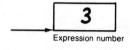

"3" is outgoing, social, animated, popular, artistic, creative, expressive, imaginative. "3" is most comfortable in cheerful, expressive, or decorative occupations.

"4" has tremendous self-discipline, is a tireless worker, obedient, enduring, persevering, sincere, honest, stubborn, conservative. "4" is most comfortable with routine and time-tested methods and is happiest building and working with material media.

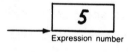

"5" is a free spirit, world traveler, entertaining, pleasure-seeking, adventurous, energetic, seeker of change. "5" is all things to all people, welcomed in any crowd. "5" succeeds best at occupations that bring him into contact with other people and allow him freedom of speech and action.

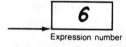

"6" is practical, stable, sentimental, home-oriented, loyal, opinionated, understanding. "6" is happiest in positions of responsibility and trust, where he can regulate, adjust, harmonize—occupations connected with homes, institutions, improving educational or material conditions, caring for the old, training the young.

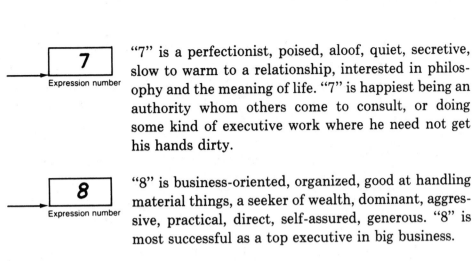

"7" is a perfectionist, poised, aloof, quiet, secretive, slow to warm to a relationship, interested in philosophy and the meaning of life. "7" is happiest being an authority whom others come to consult, or doing some kind of executive work where he need not get his hands dirty.

"8" is business-oriented, organized, good at handling material things, a seeker of wealth, dominant, aggressive, practical, direct, self-assured, generous. "8" is most successful as a top executive in big business.

"9" is a universalist, lover of mankind, has compassion for all, wants to improve conditions for humanity, searches after truth, gives freely of himself. "9" works best in occupations where the outlook is global rather than confined to small places or small situations, where inspiration, kindliness, and human understanding are essential.

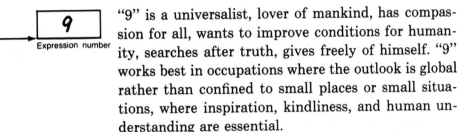

"11" is an idealist, an inspired thinker, intuitive, psychic, dramatic, vibrant, mystical, high-strung, intense, imaginative. "11" is not adapted to the business world and is happiest in a position where he can express his ideals.

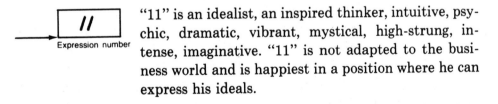

"22" is practical, resourceful, honest, warm, idealistic, inspired, a good organizer with great potential for achievement. "22" is a master builder who beautifies as he builds, who opens up new fields and makes them accessible.

7

KARMIC LESSONS

(box B—missing numerical values in name)

Karmic lessons are weak links in your character, which need to be strengthened. You do have the free will to accept or reject these lessons. However, the more you resist them, the more hard knocks and painful or annoying experiences you will receive. The weakest spot is always the hardest hit. As soon as it becomes strengthened and the lesson is learned, the strain is no longer felt.

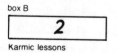

box B

1

Karmic lessons

1 is the lesson of INDIVIDUALITY. You must learn to stand alone, to think openly and freely. Until this lesson is learned, you will constantly be forced into situations where you *must* make your own decisions.

box B

2

Karmic lessons

2 is the lesson of TACT, PATIENCE, and COOPERATION. You must learn not to overlook small details. Until this lesson is learned, life will constantly force you into situations where you cannot achieve anything unless you are patient, cooperative, and observant.

box B

	3	

Karmic lessons

3 is the lesson of SELF-EXPRESSION. You must learn to have confidence in yourself. Until this lesson is learned, life will constantly force you into situations where you will lose all that you want unless you come out of your shell and express yourself openly.

box B

	4	

Karmic lessons

4 is the lesson of HARD WORK. You must learn to be patient and build sound foundations. Until you learn this lesson, life will not let you accomplish anything unless you work carefully for it. Any attempt to take short cuts or speed things along will result in loss.

box B

	5	

Karmic lessons

5 is the lesson of UNDERSTANDING and ADAPTABILITY. You must learn to be tolerant, to adapt to different situations, and above all not to be jealous or possessive of those close to you. Until this lesson is learned, life will force many changes on you and you will be faced with many crises.

box B

	6	

Karmic lessons

6 is the lesson of DOMESTIC RESPONSIBILITY. You must learn to take on responsibility willingly without seeking perfection in others. Until this lesson is learned, life will force you to make many adjustments. You will be put into situations where friends and family will do little for you yet burden you with many requirements.

box B

	7	

Karmic lessons

7 is the lesson of EMOTIONAL and SPIRITUAL MASTERY. You must learn to have faith. Until this lesson is learned you will be exposed to bereavement, loneliness, poverty, and/or isolation.

box B

8

Karmic lessons

8 is the lesson of MATERIAL AND FINANCIAL MASTERY. You must learn how to handle your own affairs. Until this lesson is learned, life will force you into situations where you must distribute your funds wisely or else feel the lack of them.

box B

9

Karmic lessons

9 is the lesson of COMPASSION. You must learn to have sympathy and understanding for the feelings of others. Until this lesson is learned life will bring you much emotional pain.

8

HIDDEN TENDENCIES

(box C—numerical categories containing 4 or more letters)

box C

/

Hidden tendencies

1 is the desire for SELF. There is a tendency to be opinionated, domineering, egotistical.

box C

2

Hidden tendencies

2 is the desire for ASSOCIATIONS. There is a tendency to rely too heavily on others, to drain family and friends both emotionally and physically.

box C

3

Hidden tendencies

3 is the desire for SELF-EXPRESSION. There is a tendency to be boastful, impatient, aimless, and party-seeking, and to scatter the energies.

box C

4

Hidden tendencies

4 is the desire to WORK. There is a tendency to smother the self with too many details and mundane tasks, to be stubborn and narrow-minded.

box C

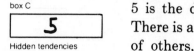

Hidden tendencies

5 is the desire for CHANGE and PERSONAL FREEDOM. There is a tendency to misuse freedom at the expense of others, to overindulge in sex or drugs, to seek change without reason, to be hasty and impulsive.

box C

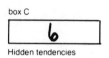

Hidden tendencies

6 is the desire for ACHIEVEMENT and RESPONSIBILITY. There is a tendency to be overly concerned with family and duties, to be stubborn, self-righteous, ingrained with unyielding ideals.

box C

Hidden tendencies

7 is the desire for WISDOM and KNOWLEDGE. There is a tendency toward secretiveness, scheming, alcoholism.

box C

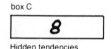

Hidden tendencies

8 is the desire for MATERIAL THINGS. There is a tendency to be overly concerned with the attainment of wealth and power.

box C

Hidden tendencies

9 is the desire for UNIVERSAL KNOWLEDGE and ALL-ENCOMPASSING LOVE. There is a tendency to be overly concerned with the problems of the world to the detriment of one's own self.

9

SUBCONSCIOUS RESPONSE

(box D: 9 – amount of karmic lessons)

box D

3

Subconscious response

"3" is a scattered, decentralized individual of ungoverned actions who reacts destructively and explosively.

box D

4

Subconscious response

"4" is lost in a maze of details. His reactions are very weak and his tendency is to vacillate.

box D

5

Subconscious response

"5" is tense and nervous. In a crisis he would be confused and impulsive.

box D

6

Subconscious response

"6" is sentimental. His first concern would be for his loved ones and prized possessions.

box D

7

Subconscious response

"7" is aloof and does not get personally involved. He would regard the situation analytically, then retreat into himself and pray. He might also turn to drink.

box D

8

Subconscious response

"8" is efficient and organized in a crisis. He is dependable and solid and can be relied upon in any situation.

box D

9

Subconscious response

"9" is bored with life. Most things are of little importance to him. In a crisis he is impersonal, philosophical, resigned.

10

DESTINY NUMBER

(box E—sum of the month, day, year of birth)

The destiny number shows the direction you *must* take, representing the only opportunities for success that will be made available to you. You would do well to choose an occupation that makes use of these opportunities, for to reject the destiny number is to court a life of frustration and disaster.

Note: If the destiny number, expression number, and motivation number are in harmony with one another, you will have little difficulty choosing your true vocation in life. If, however, these numbers are at odds with each other, what you want to do may not fit what you are actually doing, and there will be constant interferences and confusion in your plans and career.

box E

Destiny number

"1" is the destiny of ATTAINMENT and LEADERSHIP. The person with a destiny number of "1" must cultivate individuality, independence, and the ability to "go it alone."

box E

2

Destiny number

"2" is the destiny of ASSOCIATION with other people. The person with a destiny number of "2" must cultivate patience, diligence, cooperation, observation, tact, loyalty, and the ability to follow the lead of others.

box E

3

Destiny number

"3" is the destiny of SOCIABILITY. The person with a destiny number of "3" must cultivate self-expression, creativity, and social contacts.

box E

4

Destiny number

"4" is the destiny of ATTAINMENT through HARD WORK. The person with a destiny number of "4" must cultivate patience, dependability, and willing service.

box E

5

Destiny number

"5" is the destiny of FREQUENT CHANGE. The person with a destiny number of "5" must cultivate adaptability and learn responsibility and the proper use of freedom.

box E

6

Destiny number

"6" is the destiny of RESPONSIBILITY and LEADERSHIP. The person with a destiny number of "6" must learn to adjust to inharmonious conditions, assume the burdens of others, maintain his own ideals, and serve cheerfully.

box E

7

Destiny number

"7" is the destiny of WISDOM and ALONENESS. The person with a destiny number of "7" must develop his mental powers, study, meditate, search for the deeper meaning of life, become a specialist.

box E

8

Destiny number

"8" is the destiny of MATERIAL and FINANCIAL GAIN. The person with a destiny number of "8" must cultivate efficiency, business ability, and an understanding of the laws governing the accumulation, power, and use of money.

box E

9

Destiny number

"9" is the destiny of UNIVERSALITY. The person with a destiny number of "9" must SERVE and ENTERTAIN. He must learn to love his fellow man, abandon prejudices, and place others before himself.

box E

11

Destiny number

"11" is the destiny of INSPIRATION. "11" is a master number with a strong spiritual vibration. It is a number of high tension and great power. When it becomes too difficult to live with, the person may revert to "2," which is not a master number and therefore easier to handle. The person with a destiny number of "11" must investigate mysticism, trust his intuition, have faith, live humbly in the limelight, and inspire others by his own example.

box E

22

Destiny number

"22" is the destiny of the MASTER BUILDER who gives SELFLESS SERVICE TO MANKIND. "22" is a master number with a strong spiritual vibration. It is a number of high tension and great power. When it becomes too difficult to live with, the person may revert to "4," which is not a master number and is therefore easier to handle. The person with a destiny number of "22" must concern himself with humanity and use his power spiritually and idealistically.

11

LIFE CYCLES

There are three life cycles. Each cycle—for its duration—affects your destiny by representing additional circumstances and conditions that must be taken into consideration. (To find out how the various life-cycle and destiny numbers affect each other, turn to page 50 at the end of this section.)

Note: When a life cycle has the same number as one of your karmic lessons, this period will be difficult until and unless the lesson is learned.

FIRST LIFE CYCLE

(top line, box F—month of birth)

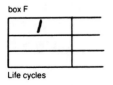

box F

Life cycles

"1" in the first life cycle marks a difficult period. The child must learn to develop his individuality. Often he is left to his own devices and given too much freedom.

2

"2" in the first cycle often indicates a badly spoiled child, or a child raised under the influence of the mother. It is a very emotional period, and the person may marry early in life.

3

"3" in the first cycle indicates a happy, carefree, social childhood. It is not especially conducive to learning, but there will probably be many opportunities for self-expression through music, art, drama, or writing.

4

"4" in the first life cycle is an indication of restrictions at home and hard work at school.

5

"5" in the first life cycle indicates many changes and a freedom that is often too great to be handled constructively. Without proper guidance the person may cause himself many problems through early indulgence in sex, alcohol, or drugs.

6

"6" in the first life cycle is an indication of a restrictive childhood, filled with duties and responsibilities. The person may marry at an early age.

7

"7" in the first life cycle marks a very difficult period. The child is withdrawn and may suffer through the lack of understanding of his parents, teachers, and peers.

box F

	8	

Life cycles

"8" in the first life cycle marks a period of achievements. It is a time for learning about the material aspects of life.

box F

	9	

Life cycles

"9" is the most difficult of all first cycles. The child has good educational opportunities, but there is a lot of tension and he feels vague, frightened, nervous, and decentralized. There is usually some loss in this cycle.

box F

	11	

Life cycles

"11" in the first life cycle is too high-powered a number for the child to cope with. It is usually reduced to a "2."

SECOND LIFE CYCLE

(middle line, box F—day of birth)

box F

	1	

Life cycles

"1" in the second life cycle marks a period of ambition, inner drive for achievement, and possible success. The person must develop his own resources and strive for independence.

box F

	2	

Life cycles

"2" in the second life cycle indicates a period of receptivity and partnerships. The person must cultivate patience, tact, and diplomacy and become aware of the feelings of other people. The person with a 2 in his middle cycle can easily have a diplomatic career.

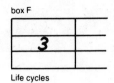

box F

3

Life cycles

"3" in the second life cycle marks a pleasant, carefree, social cycle, in which creativity and originality flourish and the person has the opportunity to express himself through art, music, drama, or writing. During this period he should develop his talents for self-expression and try not to scatter his energies.

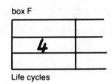

box F

4

Life cycles

"4" in the second life cycle indicates a period of hard work, productivity, and the laying of foundations. The person must learn to accept routine, work at a definite task, and practice economy.

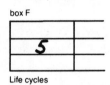

box F

5

Life cycles

"5" in the second life cycle indicates a period of expansion, travel, change, romance, freedom, and new activities and friends. Opportunities lie away from home. The person must learn to be adaptable, seek new viewpoints, and avoid the tendency to settle in one spot.

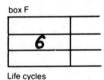

box F

6

Life cycles

"6" in the second life cycle indicates a period of adjustments and responsibilities in domestic affairs. It is the best cycle for marriage.

box F

7

Life cycles

"7" in the second life cycle indicates a period of restful growth, study, inner thought. This is not a good cycle for partnerships or marriage. The person must develop his inner resources.

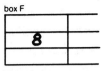

box F

Life cycles

"8" in the second cycle indicates a period of concern with the material aspects of life. The person feels driven to acquire wealth and power. In this cycle there is the possibility of great achievement in the business world.

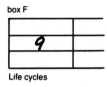

box F

Life cycles

"9" in the second cycle brings the possibility of success in public life. It is a spiritual period and the person must cultivate tolerance, love for humanity, selflessness, and emotional control. Personal love affairs do not thrive in this cycle, marriage seldom lasts, and the person usually suffers some loss.

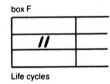

box F

Life cycles

"11" in the second life cycle marks a period of ideals, revelations, greatness, and possible fame. The person should stay away from commercial ventures and speculations. It is a time to develop the mind, become a specialist, teach, and inspire others by one's own example.

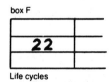

box F

Life cycles

"22" in the second life cycle brings opportunities for great achievement and top leadership. The person's aim must be to benefit humanity. Because of the high power of this number, there may be strain on the nerves and emotions during this period.

THIRD LIFE CYCLE

(bottom line, box F—year of birth)

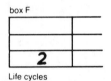

"1" in the third life cycle marks a lonely end to life. The person must remain active and independent and rely on his own resources.

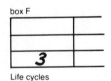

"2" in the third life cycle marks a period of warm love and close friends. The person will have the urge to collect things such as stamps, coins, antiques.

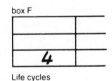

"3" in the third life cycle indicates a period of self-expression through art, music, drama, or writing. Creativity will flourish. There will be many friends and social activities.

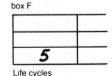

"4" in the third cycle indicates that the person will continue working—either through necessity or choice. There will be no retirement or life of ease.

"5" in the third cycle marks a period of personal freedom, travel, change, new activities, variety.

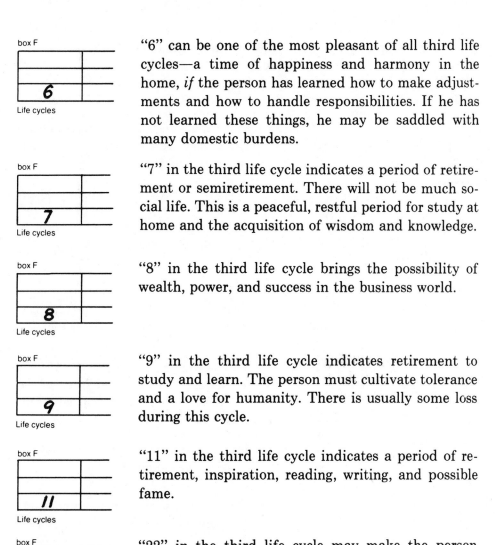

box F

Life cycles

"6" can be one of the most pleasant of all third life cycles—a time of happiness and harmony in the home, *if* the person has learned how to make adjustments and how to handle responsibilities. If he has not learned these things, he may be saddled with many domestic burdens.

box F

Life cycles

"7" in the third life cycle indicates a period of retirement or semiretirement. There will not be much social life. This is a peaceful, restful period for study at home and the acquisition of wisdom and knowledge.

box F

Life cycles

"8" in the third life cycle brings the possibility of wealth, power, and success in the business world.

box F

Life cycles

"9" in the third life cycle indicates retirement to study and learn. The person must cultivate tolerance and a love for humanity. There is usually some loss during this cycle.

box F

Life cycles

"11" in the third life cycle indicates a period of retirement, inspiration, reading, writing, and possible fame.

box F

Life cycles

"22" in the third life cycle may make the person high-strung and nervous. He should take care to keep active during this period, and take up a hobby such as sculpture.

The Effect Destiny Number and Life-Cycle Number
Have on Each Other

Destiny Number	Life-Cycle Number	Effect They Have on Each Other
1	*1*	Same numbers *intensify* each other. There may be overactivity or strain during this period.
	2	The "1" is aggressive and must stand alone, whereas the "2" is passive and seeks associations with other people. The conflict between these two numbers may cause emotional strain during this period.
	3	This is a harmonious combination, bringing with it the chance for success.
	4	The progressive, self-seeking "1" will feel hampered by the limitations of the "4." This may cause emotional strain during this period.
	5	This is a harmonious combination, bringing change into the life.
	6	This combination brings responsibilities, promotions, and love affairs into the life.
	7	The introspective "7" will slow down the life during this cycle, and it will probably be a period of seeking knowl-

Destiny Number	Life-Cycle Number	Effect They Have on Each Other

1

edge and understanding about the higher meanings of life.

8 This is a harmonious combination.

9 This is a harmonious combination, bringing the possibility of "greatness" into the life.

11 This combination can be harmonious if you are not materialistic. Otherwise there can be some emotional strain through conflict between the self-seeking "1" and the idealistic "11."

22 This is a harmonious combination.

2

1 The "1" is aggressive and must stand alone, whereas the "2" is passive and seeks associations with other people. This creates a conflict, which may lead to emotional strain during this period.

2 These numbers intensify each other. There may be poorer health or emotional upset during this period.

3 This combination is harmonious for all matters pertaining to love. In other areas, however, there is a conflict between "2's" need to be subservient, a part of the background, and "3's" need to be expressive and outgoing.

Destiny Number	Life-Cycle Number	Effect They Have on Each Other
2	4	This is a harmonious combination, but the "4" may cause some emotional limitation.
	5	"2" needs companionship, and "5" needs freedom, variety, frequent change. This combination brings into this period a tendency toward excessive sexual desires, conflicts, mistakes through wrong associations.
	6	This is a harmonious combination—especially for love affairs and domestic life.
	7	This could be a harmonious and peaceful combination. However, there may be some conflict between "2's" need for companionship and "7's" need to be alone.
	8	This is a harmonious combination.
	9	The "2" cannot be alone, and "9" hates being confined. This combination may bring some emotional upsets into the life.
	11	This is a harmonious combination.
	22	This is a harmonious combination.

Destiny Number	Life-Cycle Number	Effect They Have on Each Other
3	*1*	This is a harmonious combination bringing the chance for success into the life.
	2	This combination works harmoniously in matters pertaining to love, but there is a conflict between "2's" need to be subservient and "3's" need to be expressive and outgoing.
	3	These numbers intensify each other and may cause you to scatter your energies during this cycle.
	4	The expressive needs of "3" conflict with the limitations of "4," thus causing some emotional strain during this period.
	5	This is a harmonious combination.
	6	This is a harmonious combination.
	7	There is a conflict between the outgoing "3" and the introspective "7." During this cycle, the "7" will tone down the "3."
	8	This combination can work either way—sometimes harmoniously, sometimes at odds. Both are creative, expressive, outgoing, but "3" is pleasure-oriented and may find "8's" materialistic interests burdensome.

Destiny Number	Life-Cycle Number	Effect They Have on Each Other
3	9	This is a harmonious combination.
	11	This is a harmonious combination.
	22	This is a harmonious combination.
4	1	"1's" need to forge ahead conflicts with the limitations of "4," thus creating some emotional strain during this period.
	2	This is a harmonious combination, although there may be some feeling of emotional limitation during this period.
	3	The limitations of the hard-working "4" conflict with the expressive needs of "3," thus bringing some emotional strain into this period.
	4	These numbers intensify each other. There may be limitations and an overload of work during this cycle.
	5	Hard-working "4" has conflicting interests with freedom-loving "5," which may cause emotional strain during this period.
	6	This is a harmonious combination.
	7	This is a harmonious combination.

Destiny Number	Life-Cycle Number	Effect They Have on Each Other
4	8	This is a harmonious combination, but there is a possibility of loss or limitation during this period, as karmic debts are collected during this combination of numbers.
	9	There is a conflict between the limitations of "4" and "9's" dislike of being confined. This could cause some emotional strain. However, if "4" is involved in humanitarian work, this can be a harmonious combination.
	11	Conflict between the down-to-earth "4" and the idealistic, visionary "11" may cause emotional strain during this period.
	22	This is a harmonious combination.
5	1	This is a harmonious combination, bringing with it the possibility of attainment in this cycle.
	2	"2's" desire for companionship paired with "5's" need for freedom, change, and variety creates a period of conflicts and mistakes through wrong associations.
	3	This is a harmonious combination.
	4	Conflict between "4's" need to work and "5's" need for change and variety

Destiny Number	Life-Cycle Number	Effect They Have on Each Other

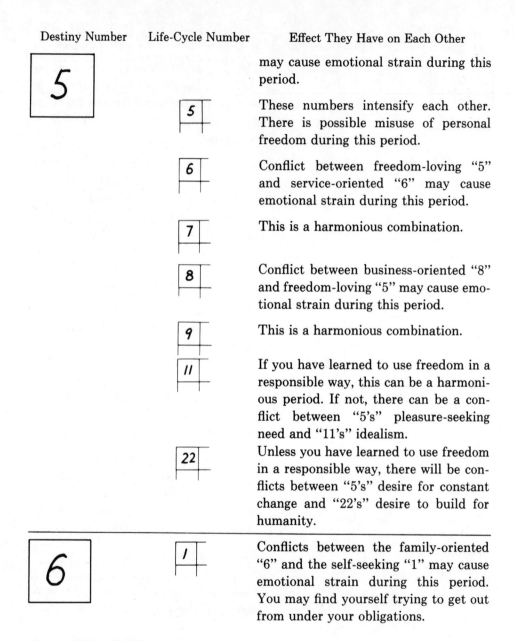

		may cause emotional strain during this period.
5	**5**	These numbers intensify each other. There is possible misuse of personal freedom during this period.
	6	Conflict between freedom-loving "5" and service-oriented "6" may cause emotional strain during this period.
	7	This is a harmonious combination.
	8	Conflict between business-oriented "8" and freedom-loving "5" may cause emotional strain during this period.
	9	This is a harmonious combination.
	11	If you have learned to use freedom in a responsible way, this can be a harmonious period. If not, there can be a conflict between "5's" pleasure-seeking need and "11's" idealism.
	22	Unless you have learned to use freedom in a responsible way, there will be conflicts between "5's" desire for constant change and "22's" desire to build for humanity.
6	**1**	Conflicts between the family-oriented "6" and the self-seeking "1" may cause emotional strain during this period. You may find yourself trying to get out from under your obligations.

Destiny Number	Life-Cycle Number	Effect They Have on Each Other
6	**2**	This is a harmonious combination.
	3	This is a harmonious combination.
	4	This is a harmonious combination.
	5	Conflict between the family-oriented "6" and freedom-loving "5" may cause emotional strain during this period.
	6	These numbers intensify each other, bringing additional responsibilities and domestic problems into this cycle.
	7	There can be some emotional strain during this period due to conflict between the family-oriented "6" and the "7's" need to be alone.
	8	This is a harmonious combination.
	9	This is a harmonious combination.
	11	This is a harmonious combination.
	22	This is a harmonious combination.
7	**1**	This is a harmonious combination. The "1" will bring uplifting change into the life during this period.

Destiny Number	Life-Cycle Number	Effect They Have on Each Other
7	2	This could be a harmonious, peaceful combination unless there is some conflict between "2's" desire for companionship and "7's" desire to be alone.
	3	This is a harmonious combination. The "3" will give "7" an uplift during this period.
	4	This is a harmonious combination.
	5	This is a harmonious combination.
	6	This combination can work either way—sometimes harmoniously, sometimes at odds. There could be some conflict between "6's" family orientation and "7's" need to be alone.
	7	These numbers intensify each other. There is a possibility of becoming too withdrawn during this period.
	8	Conflict between the spiritual "7" and the materialistic "8" may cause emotional strain and financial loss during this period.
	9	This is a harmonious combination.
	11	This is a harmonious combination.

Destiny Number	Life-Cycle Number	Effect They Have on Each Other
7	22	Conflict between the introspective "7" and the practical "22" may cause emotional strain during this period.
8	1	This is a harmonious combination, bringing into this period the possibility of success in material affairs.
	2	This is a harmonious combination.
	3	This combination can work either way—sometimes harmoniously, sometimes at odds. There could be some conflict between "8's" materialism and "3's" need for creative self-expression.
	4	This is a harmonious combination, but it marks a period when karmic debts are collected. There is a possibility of some loss or privation during this period.
	5	Conflict between business-oriented "8" and freedom-loving "5" could cause some emotional strain during this period.
	6	This could be a harmonious combination. If, however, "8" is too busy with business to take care of problems that arise at home, there is a possibility of marital problems during this cycle.
	7	Conflict between spiritual "7" and materialistic "8" may cause emotional

Destiny Number	Life-Cycle Number	Effect They Have on Each Other

8

strain and possible financial loss during this period.

8

These numbers intensify each other. There is a possibility of financial limitation or physical strain during this period.

9

Conflict between the materialistic "8" and the humanitarian "9" may cause emotional strain during this period.

11

This is a harmonious combination.

22

This is a harmonious combination.

9

1

This is a harmonious combination. There is a possibility of greatness during this cycle.

2

Conflict between "2's" passive subservience and "9's" universal outlook may cause emotional strain during this period.

3

This is a harmonious combination.

4

Conflict between the limitations of the "4" and "9's" dislike of being confined can cause emotional strain during this period.

5

This is a harmonious combination.

Destiny Number	Life-Cycle Number	Effect They Have on Each Other
9	**6**	This is a harmonious combination.
	7	This is a harmonious combination.
	8	Conflict between the materialistic "8" and humanitarian "9" may cause emotional strain during this period.
	9	These numbers intensify each other. There may be some emotional upheaval during this cycle.
	11	With this combination there is a possibility of greatness during this cycle.
	22	This is a harmonious combination.
11	**1**	This combination works harmoniously only if the "1" is not self-seeking.
	2	This is a harmonious combination.
	3	This is a harmonious combination.
	4	There may be some conflict between the hard-working "4" and the visionary "11," leading to emotional strain during this period.
	5	This combination works harmoniously only if you have learned how to use freedom properly.

Destiny Number	Life-Cycle Number	Effect They Have on Each Other
11	6	This is a harmonious combination.
	7	This is a harmonious combination.
	8	This is a harmonious combination.
	9	With this combination, there is a possibility of greatness during this cycle.
	11	These numbers intensify each other. This may create a highly charged, tense, nervous cycle.
	22	This is a harmonious combination.
22	1	This is a harmonious combination.
	2	This is a harmonious combination.
	3	This is a harmonious combination.
	4	This is a harmonious combination.
	5	This combination can work either way—sometimes harmoniously, sometimes at odds. Harmony comes when freedom is being used properly.

Destiny Number	Life-Cycle Number	Effect They Have on Each Other
22	6	This is a harmonious combination.
	7	Conflict between the introspective "7" and practical "22" may cause emotional strain during this period.
	8	This is a harmonious combination.
	9	This is a harmonious combination.
	11	This is a harmonious combination.
	22	These numbers intensify each other. There is a possibility of greatness or insanity during this period, depending on whether or not the person is capable of handling such intense vibrations. A person with this combination could achieve immortality.

12

TURNING POINTS

(box G)

There are four turning points. They represent events that may occur during the life cycle they coincide with. However, these events may only be taken advantage of while the particular turning point is in force. (To find out when a turning point is active, refer to the years written next to it in box G of the numerological chart.) The turning points also indicate what your attitude to life will be at any given time.

Note: If a turning point has the same number as your motivation number, your wants and desires will be made available to you during the years that this turning point is in force.

If a turning point has the same number as your expression number, opportunities to help you along the lines of your abilities will be made available to you during the years that this turning point is in force.

If a turning point has the same number as your destiny number, you will have many opportunities to fulfill your destiny during the years that this turning point is in force.

If a turning point has the same number as one of your karmic lessons, the years that this turning point is in force will be difficult ones and contain a lesson to be learned.

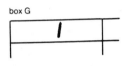

The "1" turning point is not an easy period of life. It demands courage, will, and determination. It brings opportunities to cultivate individuality, resourcefulness, and independence. Often, sudden or unexpected events will force you to stand up to life and think and act for yourself. A "1" turning point in the first life cycle may indicate a difficult, headstrong child who is hard to direct or understand.

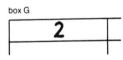

The "2" turning point brings opportunities to cultivate tact and cooperation. If you are considerate of others, this is a time of warm friends and close associations, a good time for marriage. If you are impatient or inconsiderate, it may bring difficulties in relationships and personal hurt through others. A "2" turning point in the first life cycle may indicate a strong, domineering mother or an absent father (through travel, death, divorce). The child may be oversensitive and submerge the ego.

box G

3

The "3" turning point brings opportunities to expand the social life and cultivate the talents. It is a time for self-expression, friends, romance, fertility. Careless expression of emotions may lead to unhappy experiences. Friends may be helpful but misleading. A "3" turning point in a first life cycle usually indicates a child who does not like to study. It also indicates artistic opportunities that may be wasted, causing regret later on.

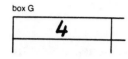

The "4" turning point brings the opportunity to build a solid foundation for the future. It is a time of hard work and limitations—patience and good work habits must be cultivated. There may be some economic problems during this period. Family and in-laws are often a responsibility. Reward comes through application and effort to get tangible results. The "4" turning point in a first life cycle often indicates that the child may go to work at an early age or that he may have many responsibilities heaped on him.

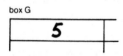

The "5" turning point brings opportunities to travel, discard the outmoded, experiment with the new. It is a time for freedom, change, and expansion, especially if it follows a "4" or a "6" turning point. A "5" turning point in a first life cycle usually indicates a child who is adventurous, restless, and lacking in application—usually making sudden changes without waiting for the reward of an effort or work to be attained.

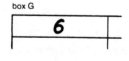

The "6" turning point brings adjustments and responsibilities, especially in the home. If you assume these willingly, this can be a period of love, domestic happiness, success, and security. If not, there will be strife, domestic burdens, and the possibility of divorce. A "6" turning point in the first life cycle usually indicates an early marriage or a responsibility to a parent, brother, or sister. When "6" is the last turning point, it can bring recognition for past work. It can also bring a single person the opportunity for love and marriage.

box G

7	

The "7" turning point is a time for introspection, meditation, and study of the deeper meanings of life. It is not a good time for marriage or partnerships. Old associations may be outgrown and left behind. You may want to withdraw into yourself, which may be misunderstood, thus causing problems in family and personal relationships. A "7" in the first life cycle usually indicates a lonely, withdrawn, studious child. It may also bring some repression into the life, such as poor health, very strict parents, or lack of money for an education. The child may be moody and develop complexes.

box G

8	

The "8" turning point brings opportunity for attainment in the business world. Expenses are high. Nevertheless, it is a time for power, recognition, and material success. An "8" turning point in a first cycle may indicate that the young person will go into business at an early age and possibly be forced to support some family member.

box G

9	

The "9" turning point brings opportunities to cultivate love, sympathy, and selflessness and to travel to foreign lands. There may be loss and disappointments in personal affairs. Success and possible fame come through humanitarian efforts during this period. A "9" in the first life cycle is hard on the child, who may have to be selfless and listen to all kinds of universal principles without receiving anything himself.

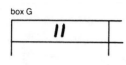

The "11" turning point may cause you to feel nervous and tense. It is a time to expand your spiritual horizons. The "11" turning point brings inspiration, illumination, and possible fame.

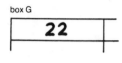

During the "22" turning point great accomplishments and tremendous creativity are possible. It is a time for international concern, world affairs, and the expansion of consciousness.

13

CHALLENGES

(boxes H and I)

There are two minor challenges (box H) and one major challenge (box I). These are the areas where you have trouble centering yourself—where you tend to go to extremes. The challenges are weaknesses to which you are prone, stumbling blocks that must be dealt with before you can attain success or happiness.

You must pay special attention to any challenge number that is the same as a life-cycle number, a turning-point number, or the destiny number. Challenges are much more difficult to deal with during these periods, and there will be much trouble in the life *until* the challenge is overcome.

When a challenge number is the same as a life-cycle or turning-point number, there could be a health problem during that period with one of the following parts of the body:

1: heart, head, emotions
2: kidneys, stomach, nerves
3: throat, liver
4: teeth, bones, circulation
5: sex organs, nerves
6: heart, neck
7: glands, nerves
8: stomach, nerves

box H

1	minor
1	minor

box I

1	MAJOR

Challenges

If you have a "1" challenge, you must learn to center yourself between having too much ego and too little ego. You must learn to be firm, assertive, self-reliant, and independent without forcing your will on others or expecting the world to revolve around you.

box H

2	minor
2	minor

box I

2	MAJOR

Challenges

If you have a "2" challenge, you may tend to be so sensitive and busy thinking about your own feelings that you are unaware of the feelings of other people. Little things are magnified out of proportion and neither forgiven nor forgotten. You must learn to stand on your own two feet, cultivate a broader outlook on life, and stop referring everything to your own feelings and emotions.

box H

3	minor
3	minor

box I

3	MAJOR

Challenges

If you have a "3" challenge, you must learn to center yourself between fearing social contacts and too much partygoing. You must learn to be social and self-expressive and to enjoy life without scattering your energies or being frivolous.

box H	
4	minor
4	minor

box I	
4	MAJOR

Challenges

box H	
5	minor
5	minor

box I	
5	MAJOR

Challenges

box H	
6	minor
6	minor

box I	
6	MAJOR

Challenges

box H	
7	minor
7	minor

box I	
7	MAJOR

Challenges

"4" is the easiest challenge of all, as there is no emotional conflict involved. You must learn to center yourself between being a "work horse" and being lazy.

If you have a "5" challenge, you must learn to center yourself between wanting too much freedom and being afraid of it altogether—between too great a lust for sensual experiences and the fear of trying new things. You must learn to restrain yourself from overindulgence in sex, drugs, and alcohol—and most difficult of all, you must learn when and how to let go of people and things that no longer serve a purpose in your life.

If you have a "6" challenge, you need to center yourself between being a "doormat" and being too exacting and domineering. You must learn to accept people as they are without expecting them to live up to your standards, respect their point of view, and not make rules for anyone except yourself.

If you have a "7" challenge, you need to center yourself between too much pride and total self-effacement. You should take care not to withdraw into yourself and seek escape from the ugly things of life through alcohol or drugs. It is especially important for you to have a good education, to learn to understand what is taking place in the world around you, to learn to give of yourself, and—above all—to have faith.

If you have an "8" challenge, you must learn to center yourself between an overconcern with material affairs and too little concern for them. You must learn the correct use of money and power and turn your thoughts to matters other than money and what it can do for you.

"0" is the challenge of choice. If you have a "0" challenge you are highly evolved and must make your own decisions about life. You must give attention to all the challenges, with no special emphasis on any particular one. You are expected to decide for yourself where your pitfalls lie.

PART III

THE YEAR AHEAD

In this section you will learn how to predict what kind of year lies ahead for you. To do this you will need to know:

1. Your personal year number.
2. What astrological influence you are under.

14

PERSONAL YEARS

Our lives operate on nine-year cycles, which keep repeating themselves. Each of these years, from 1 to 9, has its own vibration, which cannot be avoided. Each year has its own set of influences, opportunities, and obstacles. By knowing what to expect in advance, you can prepare yourself to take advantage of the opportunities and avoid the pitfalls.

Your personal year is the reduced sum of your birth month, your birth day, and the present calendar year. For example, Frank William Vilen was born on May 8. In 1978 he had a "2" personal year. $5 + 8 + 1978 = 1991 (1 + 9 + 9 + 1) = 20 = 2$.

The nine years in each cycle are very much like the stages in a harvesting season. Each one prepares for the next. In order to have a good harvest, no step can be neglected or left out.

Personal Year	Vibrations
"1" planting the seeds	This is the year for new beginnings. It is the year that sets the tone for the whole nine-year cycle. It is a time for taking the lead and showing inner strength and courage. Success and happiness come from being independent, creative, positive, selective—following your own intuitions and instincts.

The pitfall to avoid is lack of initiative, which may well result in a floundering that will continue throughout the whole cycle.

"2"
the seeds are taking root

This is the year to sit back and be patient, receptive to the ideas of others, and to remain in the background. It is a time for friendships and associations. Success and happiness come from being tactful, diplomatic, and cooperative in your dealings with other people. The pitfalls to avoid are those of being oversensitive, argumentative, and/or pushy.

"3"
first sprouts start to appear

This is a social, healthy year but can bring emotional stress. It is a time for entertaining, traveling, promoting the self, cultivating friends. Success and happiness come through being creative and through expressing words constructively—writing, lecturing, acting, singing. The pitfalls to avoid are extravagance (which can lead to financial difficulties in the "4" year) and wasting opportunities by scattering your energies. "3" is also a romance-prone year, and married people who succumb to triangle-type love affairs now may well be paving the way for a divorce or separation in the "4" year.

"4"
digging and hoeing

This is a year of limitations, hard work, and high expenses. It is a time to build for the future. Success and happiness come through self-discipline, being systematic, and putting ideas into concrete form. It is a good time to deal with property and real estate. The pitfall to avoid is that of neglecting the health—there could be some problem with teeth and/or bones.

"5"
budding time

This is the year to flow with changing conditions, to live life on a day-to-day basis, to learn to let go! It is a fast-paced, accident-prone year. It is a time of unexpected reversals—good to bad, bad to good. It is a time for fun and for short-term speculations. Success and happiness come through being adaptable, growing, expanding, promoting yourself, and picking up opportunities before they are lost. Pitfalls to avoid are those of scattering your energies, overindulging in sensual activities, and misusing your personal freedom at the expense of others.

"6"
the blossoming time

This is a year for marriage and domestic responsibilities. It is a time for domestic adjustments and obligations. It is a time when some chronic illness may come to the surface so it can be taken care of. It may be a time of travel difficulties such as car trouble, lost luggage, and so on. Success and happiness come through unselfish duty to family and community. The pitfalls to avoid are those of being overidealistic and argumentative and expecting too much from others.

"7"
the plants bear fruit

This is a year for solitude and rest. It is a time to study and perfect the inner self. It is a time for introspection. Success and happiness come through study of the deeper meanings of life. Materialistic pursuits should be avoided. Money will come in

Personal Year	Vibrations

only if not sought after. The less pushing, the greater the intake—and vice versa. The pitfalls to avoid are those of neglecting the health, forcing issues, being critical, and allowing ungrounded inner fears and complexes to arise.

"8"
the harvest time

This is a dynamic, materialistic year. Business should prosper. There can be great gain or great loss, depending on how the other years in the cycle were handled. It is an excellent time for buying and selling real estate. It is a time to pay and collect debts. Money may come from unexpected sources. Success and happiness come through thinking big, using good judgment, and being money-conscious, businesslike, efficient, and practical. Pitfalls to avoid are those of being sentimental and emotional.

"9"
time to clean up after the harvest and get ready for the new planting year

This is a cleansing year between the end of one cycle and the beginning of the next one. It is a time to get rid of anything that is unwanted or outworn—especially people who have been outgrown. It is a time for metaphysical study, writing, acting, travel. There will be some loss—a relationship may end. Success and happiness come through compassion, humanitarian efforts, being emotionally detached, and letting go of whatever starts to leave the life. Pitfalls to avoid are those of being jealous and/or possessive.

15

ASTROLOGICAL INFLUENCES

The astrological influences run in a cycle of twelve. Unlike the personal year, which is different for each person, the astrological influences are the same for all people of the same age. They spell out specific happenings and describe what your personal year will revolve around.

To find out which astrological influence you are under, refer to the table on page 82.

Frank William Vilen was under the astrological influence of "12" from his 37th birthday on May 8, 1978, until his 38th birthday on May 8, 1979. Part of this "12" influence coincided with his "2" personal year (May 8, 1978–December 31, 1978), and part of it coincided with his "3" personal year (January 1, 1979–May 7, 1979).

Astrological Influence	Where the Emphasis Is Placed
1	The emphasis is on you yourself, your personal ambitions and aspirations.
2	The emphasis is on money and personal possessions.

Astrological Influence	Ages when it occurs
1	0-1, 12-13, 24-25, 36-37, 48-49, 60-61, 72-73, 84-85
12	1-2, 13-14, 25-26, 37-38, 49-50, 61-62, 73-74, 85-86
11	2-3, 14-15, 26-27, 38-39, 50-51, 62-63, 74-75, 86-87
10	3-4, 15-16, 27-28, 39-40, 51-52, 63-64, 75-76, 87-88
9	4-5, 16-17, 28-29, 40-41, 52-53, 64-65, 76-77, 88-89
8	5-6, 17-18, 29-30, 41-42, 53-54, 65-66, 77-78, 89-90
7	6-7, 18-19, 30-31, 42-43, 54-55, 66-67, 78-79, 90-91
6	7-8, 19-20, 31-32, 43-44, 55-56, 67-68, 79-80, 91-92
5	8-9, 20-21, 32-33, 44-45, 56-57, 68-69, 80-81, 92-93
4	9-10, 21-22, 33-34, 45-46, 57-58, 69-70, 81-82, 93-94
3	10-11, 22-23, 34-35, 46-47, 58-59, 70-71, 82-83, 94-95
2	11-12, 23-24, 35-36, 47-48, 59-60, 71-72, 83-84, 95-96

Astrological Influence	Where the Emphasis Is Placed
3	The emphasis is on brothers and sisters, friends, neighbors, short trips, and communications.
4	The emphasis is on home, beginnings and endings, parents, and real estate.
5	The emphasis is on social activities, creativity, speculative ventures, romance, and pregnancy.
6	The emphasis is on health, work, pets, and employees.
7	The emphasis is on marriage and partnerships.
8	The emphasis is on property, inheritances, and sex.
9	The emphasis is on long-distance travel, publishing, litigation, philosophical studies, foreigners, and in-laws.
10	The emphasis is on career and personal reputation.
11	The emphasis is on friends, personal hopes and wishes.
12	The emphasis is on subconscious fears, behind-the-scenes activities, hospitals, and public institutions.

16

COMBINING THE TWO

Your personal year runs parallel to the calendar year (from January to December), whereas the astrological influence runs from birthday to birthday. Thus, unless your birthday falls in December or January, your astrological influence will overlap a part of two different personal years (see Frank William Vilen example on page 81).

Astrological Influence	Personal Year	Combination
1	1	If you take the initiative, you will have opportunities to advance, and help will come from other people.
	2	Appearance is important, but do not be pushy. Be patient and subservient.
	3	You can receive publicity without much effort. Projects will "click." You can influence others through social activities and self-expression.
	4	Follow through with things already started. Help will be limited.

Astrological Influence	Personal Year	Combination
1	5	Good combination for publicity, saleswork, and success in the performing and creative arts.
	6	Personal enterprises will revolve around the home.
	7	Help may come from people who appear out of your past. There may be an element of secrecy or strangeness involved.
	8	Projects move quickly toward success, and financial aid will be easy to get if you need it.
	9	This combination brings publicity.
2	1	Financial endeavors will be successful. This is a good time to start a new business or job.
	2	This combination produces financial strain. There may be loss and concern about finances.
	3	Money comes in, but there is a tendency to be extravagant.
	4	This combination creates concern over money. There may not be enough to meet your obligations and responsibilities.
	5	This combination brings about a reversal of the status quo. If the "4" year was

Astrological Influence	Personal Year	Combination
2		financially good, there may be some loss now. If the "4" year was financially difficult, there may be gain.
	6	Money comes in but will have to be spent on others—for example, paying for your child's college education.
	7	Money comes in only if not sought after. Avoid any new financial ventures.
	8	This is a good financial combination.
	9	This combination indicates a loss of money. Possessions may be sold at a loss. A lump sum may come in and be quickly dissipated.
3	1	This is a good combination for social activities, new friends, travel. There may be some stress with brothers and/or sisters.
	2	This combination is pleasant, creative, and good for group affiliations. There may be some communication telling you about a loss of some kind.
	3	This is a good combination for travel, and for promoting yourself, writing, and acting. There may be some stress with brothers and/or sisters.
	4	Travel will be limited. There may be some stress caused by problems of

Astrological Influence	Personal Year	Combination
3		brothers and/or sisters. Communications you receive may ask for help or announce a death or illness. You may do some kind of community work and not receive recognition for it.
	5	The emphasis is on travel, the unexpected, and sensual associations.
	6	There may be many demands for emotional and/or financial aid from brothers and/or sisters.
	7	The emphasis is on travel. You may receive news about the illness of someone close.
	8	Travel will be business- or career-oriented. You could become involved in some large community project. Brothers and/or sisters are likely to ask for financial aid.
	9	The emphasis is on long-distance travel and unpleasant communications.
4	1	Domestic problems may come to the foreground. An emotional relationship may end. A new home may be obtained.
	2	You will probably have some problems with a female relative. This combination sometimes indicates the death of a mother. You may have some real-estate loss.

Astrological Influence	Personal Year	Combination
4	3	This combination brings deep, heavy emotional problems with someone close to you. It could herald a forthcoming divorce or separation.
	4	Relatives may ask for emotional and/or financial aid. An elderly relative may die.
	5	This combination indicates the end of a relationship that will free you from negative circumstances.
	6	With this combination there may be heavy responsibility toward family members, which could strain your resources.
	7	You may be involved with hospitals or public institutions through a relative.
	8	You may be called to task for domestic responsibilities you neglected in years gone by—this could lead to a divorce in the "9" year.
	9	End of an emotional relationship.
5	1	Possibility of a new love affair, a new creative venture, a pregnancy.
	2	Good combination for friendship, courtship, pregnancy. There could be some deception in a romantic situation.

Astrological Influence	Personal Year	Combination
5	3	This is a social, romance-prone combination with strong pregnancy vibrations. There could be some short-lived emotional upset over a romantic situation.
	4	There will be limitations concerning romances and recreation.
	5	This is the strongest of all pregnancy vibrations. It is a good combination for creativity, amusement, and romance.
	6	Recreation will revolve around family activities. Romances will lead to marriage and probably involve some responsibility.
	7	The emphasis is on travel, hobbies, secret romances, and triangle-type love experiences.
	8	Love affairs started under this combination will probably provide financial security.
	9	The emphasis is on entertainment and travel. Love affairs will probably be emotionally upsetting and not last very long.
6	1	You may change jobs, get a new pet, or have problems with one you already own.

Astrological Influence	Personal Year	Combination
6	2	You may get a new pet or have problems with one you already own. There may be some stress with fellow workers. Watch your health.
	3	You will probably have a heavy work load and an improvement in finances. You may have some emotional upset over a pet.
	4	You may have to work hard without compensation. There may be some stress with fellow workers. There may be a problem with health.
	5	This combination indicates a change in your work.
	6	This combination brings heavy responsibilities, a heavy work load, and possible problems with pets and/or servants.
	7	There may be a health problem. You may have something stolen by an employee. There may be some under-the-surface deceit and treachery.
	8	The work load will be heavy but financially rewarding.
	9	This combination indicates the end of something—a job, a servant who may resign, a pet who may die or run away.

Astrological Influence	Personal Year	Combination
7	1	This combination usually brings marriage to single people, and the possibility of divorce to married people who are having trouble ironing out their problems.
	2	Single people may have an opportunity for marriage. Married people will have arguments and problems that could lead to separation or divorce.
	3	There will be emotional strain concerning romantic situations.
	4	Single people will probably meet their mate. Married people will have emotional stress but not necessarily a breakup in the relationship.
	5	The emphasis is on sex, romance, and short-lived arguments over sex.
	6	Single people will get married. Married people will be argument-prone, but their problems and/or separations will be patched up again.
	7	There is a tendency toward secret love affairs. Married people may feel upset with each other but hold it in and build up resentments.
	8	Single people may meet a financially well-off mate. Married people who have

Astrological Influence	Personal Year	Combination
7		been having problems may separate or divorce.
	9	This combination brings an end to marriage and romance.
8	1	You may receive money from an unexpected source. Women should have a complete physical checkup.
	2	You may receive some unexpected money. An elderly female relative may die.
	3	You may have some sexually triggered emotional problems.
	4	You may have a struggle over joint ownership of some property. There is a possibility that you may have an accident or be mugged.
	5	There may be large financial gains—unexpected windfalls. Sex problems may cause emotional stress.
	6	This combination usually results in the joint-ownership type of purchase of a house or some property. You may receive an inheritance. There may be some sexual problems.
	7	There may be a physical problem involving a sex organ. A relative may die. You may receive a large amount of unexpected money.

Astrological Influence	Personal Year	Combination
8	8	You may receive an inheritance. You may have an emotional or physical sex-related problem. You may receive money from some strange unexpected source.
	9	A relative may die. You may have some problem over the joint ownership of some property. You may have some emotional sex-related problem.
9	1	There is a possibility of holding public office, or having something published, of long-distance travel, of successful litigation, of a romance with a foreigner, of becoming interested in a study of metaphysics.
	2	This is a romance-prone combination. There may be some mother-in-law problems.
	3	This combination brings the chance of having something published, travel, successful litigation, and some problems with brothers- and/or sisters-in-law.
	4	Heavy stress with in-laws. Any litigation under this combination will probably have a negative outcome.
	5	Emphasis is on long-distance travel, publicity, successful litigation, short-lived romances.

Astrological Influence	Personal Year	Combination
9	6	In-laws may make financial and emotional demands. Any romance that starts now will probably last.
	7	Emphasis is on an inner search for wisdom.
	8	Emphasis is on successful litigation, long-distance business transactions, and having things published that are of a business nature.
	9	Emphasis is on a study of religion and/or philosophy, long-distance travel, and short-lived romance. There may be some stress caused by in-laws.
10	1	This is a time of advancement. There may be a job change for the better.
	2	This can be a smooth combination provided you do not push yourself and remain in the background.
	3	This combination brings the possibility of great forward strides in your career.
	4	You may have some concern over your parents.
	5	This is an erratic combination with unexpected ups and downs.
	6	Delinquent bills will have to be paid under this combination.

Astrological Influence	Personal Year	Combination
10	**7**	Try not to be overcritical during this combination.
	8	This combination can bring beneficial business contacts.
	9	There may be some legal problems. It is, however, a good combination for acting, teaching, and writing.
11	**1**	Help will come from outside sources, and you will have the opportunity to fulfill your hopes and wishes. There is a possibility of recognition and/or fame.
	2	There may be some setback in your hopes and wishes, but you will make new friends and contacts.
	3	This is a good time for social activity and promoting yourself.
	4	You may have some disappointments involving friends, hopes, and/or wishes.
	5	Success in any area involving the performing arts, sales, travel.
	6	Your hopes and wishes may center around your home.
	7	You may withdraw from your friends and become interested in inner development.

Astrological Influence	Personal Year	Combination
11	8	You may have financial gain through friends.
	9	Friends may leave your life, or there may be a disappointment concerning some hope or wish that will collapse.
12	1	If you have carried over problems that should have been let go of in the "9" year, you may be depressed and suffer from subconscious fears that need to be brought under control.
	2	This period could bring secret love affairs, negative involvements with hospitals or public institutions, problems involving women, or underhanded behind-the-scenes actions by enemies. It is a stressful time.
	3	There could be a separation or divorce, which may lead to legal problems. Mental stress with loved ones is due to your own shortcomings. There may be a secret love relationship.
	4	Health may be a problem.
	5	There may be a love affair that will involve some kind of deception or secrecy. You may have some legal involvement.
	6	This is a time of domestic stress and

Astrological Influence	Personal Year	Combination
12		possibly divorce. Someone you are responsible for may need medical care.
	7	There is a possibility of ill health and/or hospitalization.
	8	You may do some work behind the scenes. You may have some legal problems.
	9	This is a period of great loss and/or suffering.

BIBLIOGRAPHY

Arroyo, Stephen. *Astrology, Psychology and the Four Elements*. Davis, Cal.: CRCS Publications, 1975.

Avery, Kevin Quinn. *The Numbers of Life*. Garden City, N.Y.: Doubleday, 1977.

Campbell, Florence. *Your Days Are Numbered*. Ferndale, Pa.: The Gateway, 1976.

Cheiro. *Cheiro's Book of Numbers*. New York: ARCO, 1976.

Goodwin, Matthew Oliver. *Numerology, The Complete Guide*, Vols. I and II. No. Hollywood, Cal.: Newcastle, 1981.

Haich, Elisabeth. *Yoga and Destiny*. New York: ASI, 1977.

Hook, Dianna farington. *The I Ching and You*. New York: E. P. Dutton, 1973.

_____. *The I Ching and Mankind*. London: Routledge & Kegan Paul, 1975.

Jordan, Dr. Juno. *Numerology: The Romance in Your Name*. Marina del Rey, Cal.: DeVorss, 1977.

Jung, Carl G. *Synchronicity*. Princeton, N.J.: Princeton University Press, 1973.

Lovell, Rev. Elois Winkler. *Wisdom of the Tarot Taught Simply*. Van Nuys, Cal.: Astro-Analytics Publications, 1978.

Macleod, Charlotte. *Astrology for Skeptics*. New York: Macmillan, 1972.

Progoff, Ira. *Jung, Synchronicity and Human Destiny*. New York: Dell, 1973.

Sepharial. *The Kabala of Numbers*. No. Hollywood, Cal.: Newcastle, 1974.

Seton, Julia, M.D. *Symbols of Numerology*. No. Hollywood, Cal.: Newcastle, 1984.

Weingarten, Henry. *A Modern Introduction to Astrology*. New York: ASI, 1974.

ABOUT THE AUTHOR

In keeping with her "9" first life cycle, Sandra Stein started life in Calcutta, India, traveled the world, and ended up in Montreal, Canada, where she received her B.A. from McGill University and her M.A. from the University of Montreal. She then tried her hand in many areas, ranging from art to speech pathology, from computer programing to marriage.

Sandra Stein now lives in New York with her two children, and—having finally chosen to follow her destiny number of "7"—is deeply involved in the study of astrology and numerology.

This handbook came about through frustration at not being able to grasp everything she was reading fast enough to suit her, and at not being able to find a ready-made work sheet to put her charts on. She finally decided to design her own work sheet and to write her own handbook in which she synthesizes and classifies the basics of what she has read into a clear, handy format.

Letter values		
1	A	J	S
2	B	K	T
3	C	L	U
4	D	M	V
5	E	N	W
6	F	O	X
7	G	P	Y
8	H	Q	Z
9	I	R	

Letter values

line 1
Vowels

line 2
Name

line 3
Consonants

line 4
Total

box A

1	
2	
3	
4	
5	
6	
7	
8	
9	

Total letters in
each number

box B

Karmic lessons

line 5

Month

Day

Year of Birth

box E

Destiny
number

box F

Life cycles   Years

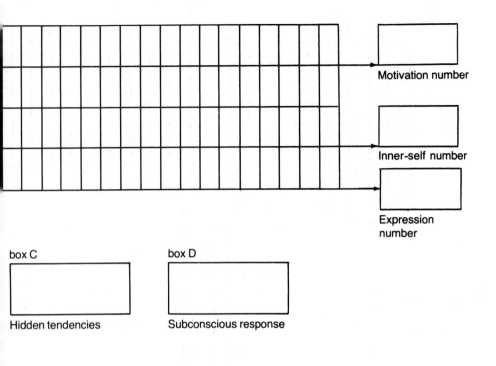

Motivation number

Inner-self number

Expression
number

box C

Hidden tendencies

box D

Subconscious response

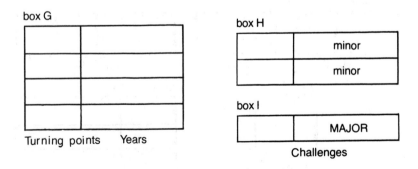

box G

Turning points   Years

box H

	minor
	minor

box I

	MAJOR

Challenges

1	A	J	S
2	B	K	T
3	C	L	U
4	D	M	V
5	E	N	W
6	F	O	X
7	G	P	Y
8	H	Q	Z
9	I	R	

Letter values

line 1
Vowels

line 2
Name

line 3
Consonants

line 4
Total

box A

1	
2	
3	
4	
5	
6	
7	
8	
9	

Total letters in
each number

box B

Karmic lessons

line 5

Month

Day

Year of Birth

box E

Destiny
number

box F

Life cycles   Years

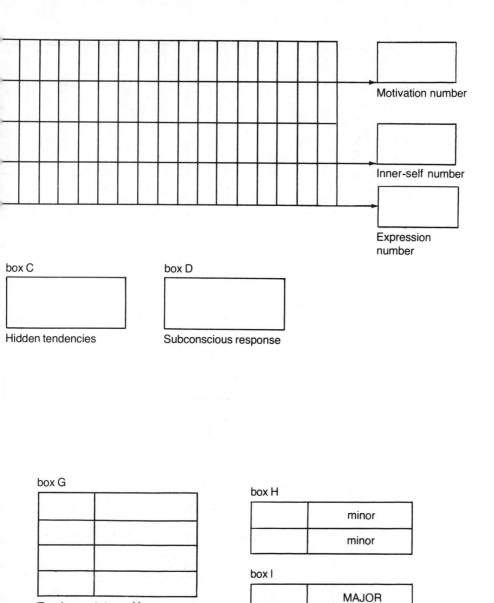

Motivation number

Inner-self number

Expression
number

box C

Hidden tendencies

box D

Subconscious response

box G

Turning points   Years

box H

	minor
	minor

box I

	MAJOR

Challenges

Letter values					
1	A	J	S		line 1 Vowels
2	B	K	T		
3	C	L	U		line 2 Name
4	D	M	V		
5	E	N	W		line 3 Consonants
6	F	O	X		
7	G	P	Y		line 4 Total
8	H	Q	Z		
9	I	R			

Letter values

box A

1	
2	
3	
4	
5	
6	
7	
8	
9	

Total letters in
each number

box B

Karmic lessons

line 5

Month   Day   Year of Birth

box E

Destiny
number

box F

Life cycles   Years

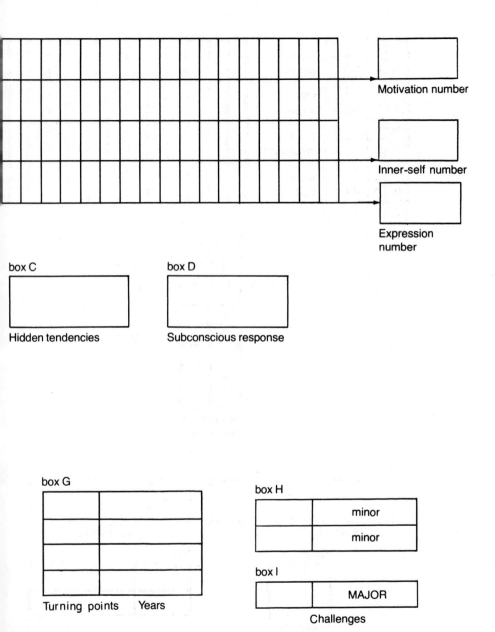

Motivation number

Inner-self number

Expression
number

box C

Hidden tendencies

box D

Subconscious response

box G

Turning points   Years

box H

	minor
	minor

box I

	MAJOR

Challenges

1	A	J	S
2	B	K	T
3	C	L	U
4	D	M	V
5	E	N	W
6	F	O	X
7	G	P	Y
8	H	Q	Z
9	I	R	

Letter values

line 1
Vowels

line 2
Name

line 3
Consonants

line 4
Total

box A

1	
2	
3	
4	
5	
6	
7	
8	
9	

Total letters in
each number

box B

Karmic lessons

line 5

Month

Day

Year of Birth

box E

Destiny
number

box F

Life cycles   Years

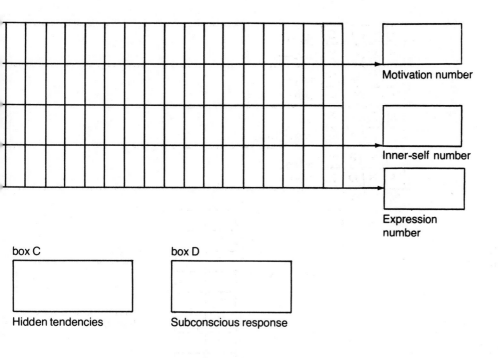

Motivation number

Inner-self number

Expression
number

box C

Hidden tendencies

box D

Subconscious response

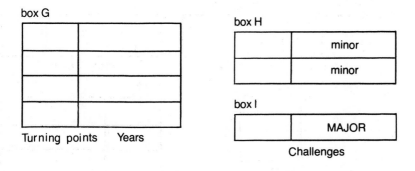

box G

Turning points   Years

box H

	minor
	minor

box I

	MAJOR

Challenges

1	A	J	S
2	B	K	T
3	C	L	U
4	D	M	V
5	E	N	W
6	F	O	X
7	G	P	Y
8	H	Q	Z
9	I	R	

Letter values

line 1 Vowels

line 2 Name

line 3 Consonants

line 4 Total

box A

1	
2	
3	
4	
5	
6	
7	
8	
9	

Total letters in each number

box B

Karmic lessons

line 5

Month

Day

Year of Birth

box E

Destiny number

box F

Life cycles   Years

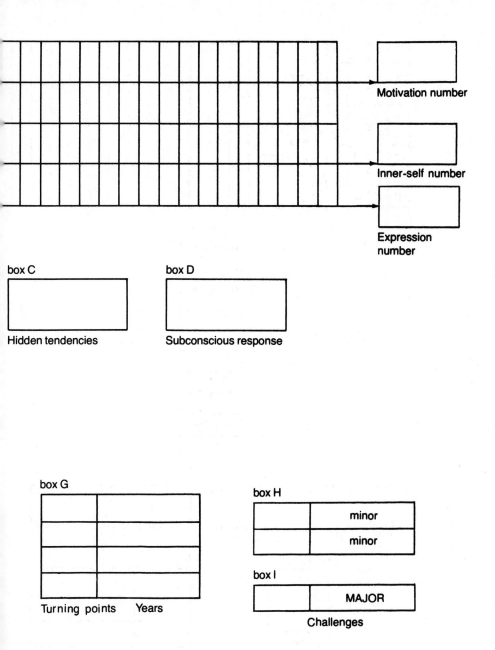

Motivation number

Inner-self number

Expression
number

box C

Hidden tendencies

box D

Subconscious response

box G

Turning points   Years

box H

	minor
	minor

box I

	MAJOR

Challenges